monarch

monarch

poetry for the seeker

Shelah Rochelle Ott

dedication

to the ones I love—monarch butterflies and all.

content

acknowledgments

My deepest gratitude to Tessa Wiley for her beautiful cover art, to my incredible life coach Amber, and to my amazing family and friends for their constant support and love.

preface

Self-expression is an aspect of creation: the life-force that lies behind everyone and everything. I wrote these poems through my deepest struggles, where I also found my greatest love. They are meant to be kind guides for loving wider, digging deeper, healing wounds that need it—especially when you didn't know they were there—and discovering the deepest love for your self and for life. This love will carry you from the deepest, darkest moments of your life, all the way through the moments of pure joy. It is always there. All you must do is seek it, enjoy the unfolding, and remember that you are, in essence, divinity.

birth

sometimes when a girl
gets into your car
and she emanates warm vanilla and lavender
she isn't doing it for your enjoyment
but for her own

because at times she wants to smell lovely
just because
or wear clothes that hug her skin beautifully
just because

or maybe it's because women
are not always seeking the attention of men
maybe they're just seeking strength from within
in the form of pleasant things
that just so happen
to please you

and maybe she does need you
not to have your hand
down her pants
or your tongue
down her throat
when you think she wants it

but maybe what she needs
is you to move your mouth

in the shape of words
and offer kindness in your eyes
when you know she needs it

don't
for a second
think the words rolling off of your
tongue
are too much

you were made with a fire
in your being
never to be put out
by the demands of a man's world

baby,
believe me when I say
there ain't nothing in this world
more magical
than the swing of those hips
you think are too wide
and the softness of your belly
that you wish wasn't there

and don't you ever
forget
that the tired hands
of your own mother
are the product of hours spent
planting a seed
and giving it everything possible
so it could grow roots deep

while reaching towards
the sun

dear future children:

hi baby,

I really did try.
if you were alive then
you could see the look
in all of our eyes
you could feel the pain
we were all feeling inside
when we clicked on the news
and found another species
had died.

trust me,
we tried.

did you know there were polar bears?
did you know there were bees?
that some of the most incredible species
no longer breathe?

we witnessed it happen
and we fought,
we tried.

I'm sorry it wasn't enough,
I'm sorry we had a government
that was too blind to see
the worth that lies
behind every body
every being

and now we're handing down
the mess that we've made
without much of a reason
than power and getting
paid.

I promise you,
it was beautiful
the life that we lived
despite all of the struggle
we found hope
and love to give.

I know things are different now
and it kills me inside
but baby,
I just wanted to let you know,
we really did try.

love, mom

heartbreaking
how I let the harshness
of others
push me miles away
from knowing my roots
and now my heart
is craving
to know the tongue of
my mother
and the brown-skinned land
of her youth

I numbed my mind
to be in the presence
of boys
I didn't even like
seeking my strength
in empty places
when I just needed
to look inside

loving you is like
remembering who I was
before the world
hardened me

the insides of my
thighs
seem to know when I
look into your
eyes
it's as if my whole
body
speaks
a language you taught me

those three words
taste sweeter
when you
are the reason
I speak them

caterpillar

I felt my heart
breaking
as I asked for
a sign

surrender

the universe
replied

I promise you
this is a miracle
it is simply
in disguise

exhausted
by my own mind
at the end of the night
I remind her—

give yourself
time.
trees cannot root
deep into the earth overnight

I was brought down
to my hands and knees
my body in the shape
of heartbreak
not knowing
I was carving out space
to let my heart
breathe

breathing through the breaking
I found unconditional love

denying the truth
only prolongs the
pain—
let it stay.
trust me,
my love
there is unforeseen
beauty
on its way

and I realized
through the salt water
pouring from my eyes
you can never know
another's soul
as intimately as
your own

I will never.
deny
this love
again

to give someone else
the job of filling you up—
what a heavy burden to place
on the one you love

I'm sorry for all the times
your love wasn't enough
unconditional always
yet I didn't even see you,
my love

I know you've been here
since I entered this world
I guess I'm just upset
that this is how we
raise girls

where do we find it?
that love that we seek?
it's not in the men
or women of our bedsheets

I guess the only place
that we have left to look
is the one that's been whispering
since the first breath that
we took

to take
your greatest pain
and ask what purpose
it serves in your strength—
this is how
miracles
are made

innumerable nights
I spent seeking
for that missing
piece

but all the while
I was whole—
only avoiding
the journey

breaths for the times
I chose not to love me
breaths for the times
I chose inauthenticity
breaths for the times
I wanted to get out of my own skin
breaths for the times
I avoided looking within
breaths.
and breaths.
and breaths.
I will love
myself
until there are no more breaths
left

love,
let out
your cry
but remember
you are the silent strength
of the hills
rolling for miles
you are as endless
as the air
that comprises
the sky—
just wait
you will see
over time

I've climbed
this mountain before.
but just because I have
does not mean
I won't be sore

I must breathe
the air in
I must feel every inch
of strength
buried within
I must look
to the sun
in the sky
drinking her fire
through my skin
and my eyes
and remember
that I have been here
before.

I no longer blame
my mother
because just as
the women who came before her
she learned
she wasn't worth it
all of the joy
she couldn't see
all of the freedom
she wanted to be
all of the what ifs
that stayed
what could be.

the
deny ourselves
of what we crave.

the
only give love
to the children we make.

the
refusing to see
ourselves in the light
we shine on others

barely even seeing ourselves
as mothers

I began to listen
and started to see
years of darkness
find their light
within me

chrysalis

letting go
is just a side
of letting in

make space for the new
and breathe out
what you can no longer
hold in

I decided I am done
falling in love
I am through
waiting
for someone else
to pull me up
instead
I will rise
in love
I will drink it in
I will let it soak
in every inch of my skin
I will know
I am worth it
I will never forget
that I deserve it
and I will never again
naively believe
that someone else's heart
will give you all
you ever need

and when I lose sight
of my way
and my why
I remember
the same intelligence
that creates the roots of trees
put its love
into making my being

life
cannot be
insignificant

we must
be willing
to love deep enough
to rediscover our purpose

you cannot rush
a flower's bloom
no matter how badly
you wish to see
her vibrant hues

so you,
my love
why the need
for life to happen
so soon?

give yourself
permission
to fully
be
that sacred
act
sets your soul
free

I was grasping
for control
until I was gasping
for air
exhausted
just enough
to see letting go
will take me there

love
is expanding

so vast

that you release
what you can no longer
breathe

needing healing
does not mean
you are broken.
it means you are the culmination
of your environment
and those
who came before you

it means you have the blood
of warriors
and the wisdom
of sages
it means you carry the wounds
that have been lived
for ages

and although
you are not broken
you must
break open—

allow the light in
to alchemize your pain
and watch yourself grow
like seeds planted
in the springtime rain

I looked myself
in the mirror
and for the first
time
I told her
I loved her
and years of sadness
met the light

let your wounds
hold you
understand
their roots
and listen for
the wisdom
they are trying
to give you

you are your own greatest teacher
stay grounded
in your truths

and even in the deepest trenches
where I found my greatest pain

gratitude remained

and every time
I look to myself
for the strength
that has yet
to be
seen
I fall a little more
in love with
me
and recreating
the fire
that makes up
my being

the simplest
power
is the power
of thoughts—
breathe this in
and watch as your life
unbecomes
what it's not

and although
darkness can feel
like the end
just know
that a new you
is breaking out
buried
from deep within

monarch

a caterpillar does not have to think
about morphing into a butterfly
a butterfly does not have to think
about migrating south
just as you, my love
don't have to second guess
the divinity
that is itching
to come out

I refuse to build
boxes around my being
I am infinite—
no amount of space
can hold me

you are the blossoming spring time
and the sacred work of bees
carrying magic
and leaving it where it is needed

you are the golden summer haze
and the cleansing power of the sea
constantly renewing
with depths farther than the eyes can see

you are the glitter of winter snow
you are the smell of autumn rain
you are miraculously here
hurling through infinite space

do not forget

you are worthy
in infinite ways

there is wisdom
in the wildflowers
sprouting between
the cracks
they tell us that
home
is our willingness
to grow
despite what may have happened
in our past

I've learned
that to live
for another's love
isn't to live
at all
because until you've loved
your own heart
you will never find
the freedom
of a love
with no walls

I have tried
and tried
to describe
our love
a thousand times
and while each depiction
paints a picture
of beautiful skies

free
and breathtaking
limitless
and wide

it will never
do justice
to what lives
inside

thank you
for building
a home with me
thank you
for making
me feel seen

when concrete is built
over the roots of a tree
it does not think
maybe this life
isn't for me.
maybe I should let
my lungs
collapse beneath me.
no—
it reaches further
for drops of water
it branches out
towards the sunlight
with persistence
and patience
morning and night
it continues to create
life on earth.
despite all of the depths
it must grow through
first

trust me
my love
you are wiser than
you think
your heart knows
where to take you
like the skies know
the green

I finally had enough
of tearing down
my own house

these hands
were not meant
to destroy
it's foundation
so instead
I began building

I colored the walls
with acts of self love
I painted the ceilings
to match the sky above
me—
a daily reminder.

that my abilities
are endless
that I am a home
for creation
that I move
and sway in
the rhythms
of the winds
that I am so vast

no eyes
can perceive
my ends

I will build
this house up
because I refuse
to let her
crumble
again

for a second
she forgot who
she was
and then she remembered

I am love

I know my breath
doesn't need yours
in order to survive
just like
my mouth
don't need to feel yours
in order to smile

but without them
life wouldn't be
the same ride

it would have a little
less color
and a little
less shine
it would be
a little rougher
and a little
more tired
it would be
less sweet
and definitely
less wide
so thank you
for helping me know
more life

I remembered where I came from
as I danced around
the room
immersed in all of the magic
my bones were craving
to live through

I got tired
of waiting for the light
to come

then I realized
I must be
my own sun

migration

I grew wings
as wide as angels
and off
I flew
when I gave myself
permission
to live out
my truth

do not forget
that you are a teacher.
a lover.
a healer.
that all of the truths
you seek to know
already lay
within your own soul

now I know
that this body
is a home—
all those times
I craved another
I was really craving
my own

I thought the world
of others
who thought the worst
of me

yet now I know
the world was teaching me
how to love
unconditionally

forgiveness
is an aged medicine
that will never lose
its potency

for yourself
and for others—
heal your wounds—
let yourself
be free

your arms
wrapped around me
softly putting me
to sleep
like the raindrops
outside
wiping the earth
clean
carry me
into my dreams
and then
I wake
to find
your lips
kissing
my face—
another dream.
yet real
here
with me.

you already are
what you wish
to be

your only job
is to remove the barriers
that block your eyes
from seeing

peeling back the layers
is a life-long
journey
enjoy
it's sweet
complexity

the universe
is not simply
the skies
the universe
is not just
the unreachable
stars
scattered high
the universe
is inside of you
the universe
is love
and love
has created everything—
what is below
and what is above

to the women
that give
and give
and give

know that to receive
the warm glow
of your own
inner home

is to taste
the sweetest juice
your tongue
has ever known

sweet love,
get quiet
let your wisdom
speak

she will guide you through
the valleys
and carry you to
the peaks

I gave away
my power
for far too long

I am done denying
it's existence
when I know by nature
I am strong

I am built
to birth
life from intent

I was born to create
and move in a dance
free
from discontent

I am here
to express
life through my own lens
from love
with patience
to be the beauty
I was meant

pictures from the times
where I thought the harshest
words
and yet looking back
all I see is
beauty
within her

all wounds will heal
if you let them

I no longer fear
life's ebbs and flows
I welcome in
its magic
and the beauty
of the unknown

the willingness to love
all parts
of your being—
especially the ones
you wish
not to see—
this.
is the strength
waiting
to be let free

a note from the author

    Monarch butterflies are a beautiful species that are currently endangered. Because they are an indicator species, their decline is a loud signal that the health of our shared environment is a great concern. We can plant milkweed to assist in the growth of the species, along with purchasing organic foods and donating to non-profit organizations that protect and improve our environment.

    We share this beautiful planet with so many other species and sadly, we have come to a point where our actions as a collective are putting the entire planet's future at stake. Island nations, indigenous nationalities, and low-income communities of color are already seeing the effects of global warming, amongst billions of non-human species that we live with. Along with institutional change, as individuals we each hold tremendous power to ensure the vitality of this planet for generations to come. Moving towards zero-waste living, shopping locally and buying organic, and reducing your carbon footprint by reducing intake of meat can help co-create a healthier future for all.

    Spreading awareness creates ripples of change because this issue is not political—it is an issue that affects life as we know it. And along the way, you will discover beautiful connections to this planet that increase your capacity to love and live in the moment, appreciating the beauty that lies within our shared home.

Made in the USA
San Bernardino, CA
30 March 2019